CHAD HEDGER AND FRIENDS

CHAD HEDGER AND FRIENDS

PAUL BINDING

Shoestring Press

All rights reserved. No part of this work covered by the copyright herein may be reproduced or used in any means—graphic, electronic, or mechanical, including copying, recording, taping, or information storage and retrieval systems—without written permission of the publisher.

Printed by imprintdigital
Upton Pyne, Exeter
www.digital.imprint.co.uk

Typesetting and cover design by narrator
www.narrator.me.uk
info@narrator.me.uk
033 022 300 39

Published by Shoestring Press
19 Devonshire Avenue, Beeston, Nottingham, NG9 1BS
(0115) 925 1827
www.shoestringpress.co.uk

First published 2019
© Copyright: Paul Binding
© Cover photo by Leio McLaren (@leiomclaren) on Unsplash

The moral right of the author has been asserted.

ISBN 978-1-912524-30-3

ACKNOWLEDGMENTS

The poems 'Etruscan Witness' and 'Solitude: an Ambiguity' appeared in somewhat different forms in *Ambit Issue 184 Spring 2006*.

For Tim and Celia, Chloe and Tom

CONTENTS

They'd Sit There…	1
Chad Hedger (1)	2
Chad Hedger (2)	4
Amours de Voyage (1978)	6
Chad Hedger (3)	8
Interlude	10
… and Friends (1)	12
Chad Hedger and Friends	15
… and Friends (2)	19
Etruscan Witness	21
Solitude: An Ambiguity	23
An Irish Airman Foresees His Death by W.B. Yeats	24

THEY'D SIT THERE…

(after Henrik Ibsen "De sad der….")

They'd sit there in the cosiest house, those two,
all during autumn and long winter weather;
then the house burnt down, gutted through and through;
now the pair has to rake the ashes together.

Somewhere among these a jewel lies hidden,
a jewel which can never burn.
If they searched in earnest, it could easily happen
that *he* found it, or *she* did, in surreptitious turn.

But if this fire-fraught couple managed to find
the priceless, fireproof jewel,
she'd never recover the faith burnt from her mind,
nor he his need to defy, when life is cruel.

CHAD HEDGER (1)

'Folk just don't understand
my kind of emptiness,
they simply don't get it!
They think of emptiness
as what you find
when you open a box
and see it's got nothing inside it.
But for me emptiness
is what I'm holding
any given moment.
What I never manage to find
is the box.'
                His narrow brown eyes
in freckled face pierce my head.
'Funny,' I tell him, 'only the other day
I was thinking about you…' or rather
a 'you' who's long teased my mind,
                        Hedger, Chad Hedger:
a bright foreign river carrying a raft
over rapids beneath scorching sun,
the two of us riding it and paying
a price; a season later, one winter's morning,
you shambling up to my desk and asking,
forthright but awkward, if truly I thought
'a lonely impulse of delight' worth living for,
(was 'dying for' what you were trying to say?)
like 'that Irish airman you read about with us!'

But Chad's revenant 's jerking a thumb towards
the famous castle at our street's far end,
red sandstone against the washed-blue sky.
'We don't need that old heap
of rubbish any more, do we? No fucking use
as protection. It's all drones now, isn't it?
Fingers on keyboard and zzz, off they zoom
till phttt, houses crash and the guys in 'em fry!

Easy-peasy, not like those hard old
days when blokes flew through hell
and sometimes 'd get gongs for doing so.'
                    'But Hedger,' I say,
'Chad Hedger,' as if still on that raft....
'Do you *mind*, mate!' It's the petulant
voice of someone quite else; I've been
speaking to air, and not for the first time.
'We're aiming to get to your castle which is
English Heritage in case you didn't know.
You trying to block our way there or what?'

CHAD HEDGER (2)

Behind that famous castle—its sandstone soaked
in late summer sun, no old warfare palpable—
I find myself a rusty, unoccupied seat,
and hope the two tottering oldies
peering down at railway and river below
and the bare-armed youths flaunting
runic tattoos won't bother to join me!

Hadn't Chad—
for he *was* Chad , I'm sure—
been telling me,
through cocky negatives,
that I was not so unlike
that box he could never find?

Onto a large dock-leaf some six inches
from my left foot a butterfly
is landing. Alone. A Small Copper judging
by the black spots (eight could I
count them) on each coppery forewing,
a brilliance even in the afternoon
sun-glow. Undersides—revealed now
as it starts unfolding its confident self—
a pale orange with black spots repeated.
But it doesn't close up, not completely,
it wants to bask, part-open, on the leaf,
with space, if only narrow, between

its double-paired wings. Space but not
emptiness! For see how the spots on forewings
and the copper sheen on hindwings'
grey margins gleam through unhindered.

A second butterfly—Small Copper too,
with sex untellable—lightly judders down
through quivering inches of heat to the
same succulent dock. Soon it'll promote
a dance of relationship, finding the vacuums
it encounters no more alien than what
its bulbous eyes and its long tongue
are familiar with on growth and ground.

The Small Copper lives three weeks at most:
after my pair two entire breeds will follow,
until, in the spring, they morph into memories.

AMOURS DE VOYAGE (1978)

'I'm a Pan-worshipper!' she laughs,
skipping off the Greyhound bus into
the warm green Tennessee night,
'my father was a hero, see, a brave man—
He died a hero's death. In 'Nam!'
                              'Where else?'
sneers the passenger at my side.
'Some heroes those guys! Off their skulls
on shit the whole damn' time!'
                              'I'm Siobhan!'
she calls out, 'and it's S.I.O.B.H.A.N.—
my dad wouldn't spell me anyways different.'

Half the males on this bus have, these last
dark, knee-cramping hours, fallen in love with her,
so now we all troop after her as she frolics
her route towards Sprites and Dr Peppers,
hair russet, face tan-brown in roadside neon,
diaphanous dress floating her contented flesh
across the yard. Behind us deodorant sprays
are purging our Greyhound of human presence.
This little liberty of Space relieves us from
Time as well, in a frame of thick-wooded hills.

'Siobhan!' Speaker runs urgently through warmth;
he's young in shiny cheap black suit. 'We gotta talk!
I don't know about Pan, but I know that *Jesus* lives,
lives right here. I'm his witness, see!'
                              Right here
is no 'here' for me, I pause to think,
though can't for the moment bring back my own
real 'here', with its well-ordered contexts
for fair debate and reasonable love.
Imagine vanishing through the bus-park's
frame, letting one's very being slip between
all the oaks and sugar maples, Carolina silver-bells

and yellow buck-eyes! Imagine each of those
past-life programmes I've made for myself
dissolving into deciduous darkness,
becoming one with some dead soldier's creed
learned in 'Nam or some young missionary's
endeavour to 'save' a passing girl!
                              'You like
Root Beer, Mr Englishman?' It's
S.I.O.B.H.A.N. herself asking me a question,
and I find, of course, that, at least right now, I do.

CHAD HEDGER (3)

'And he was robust too,' I say—we're
speaking of Chad Hedger at last,
fumbling round words that establish
him not merely as dead but as having
chosen to die. I despise the adjective
that issued so unnaturally out of me,
though maybe Chad wouldn't have. Yet when
my friend of this reunion, driving his old
light-blue Merc through the little old city
of our pasts, contradicts, I'm pleased. 'Robust?
Nobody's that—can't be, once you see that
what's possible is endless.' And he should know,
who's brought medical aid to Middle East wars,
seen no-man's-lands explode with bodies,
burnt ground throwing up burnt flesh
to fire the blankness of the sky.

Low grey-stone slate-roofed houses, gardens
spraying out cotoneaster, with berries
like hundreds-and-thousands at a children's
party; wet, turned leaves on cobbled
stretches of street, and some way ahead
the cathedral, a dark, three-towered mass
solid above the shallow, bubbling river.

After my wrong word, right ones have to come,
and what will they sound like—for I must respect
both what's tough and what's vulnerable—
to my driver, for whom Chad was a mate,
and to the old blind man, former teacher
who, half a century ago, organised
a party of young (Chad and me included)
to Cold War Poland, and now cherishes the recall?

'We were both (can you see us?) fair-haired, fair-skinned.
It was the daftest thing ever for the pair of us to strip
on that raft, on that river, under that sun,
just after midday, on the Dunajec.... At the end
of our journey we all clambered off our log-
flotilla and alighted at a little spa,
(its name was Szczawnica) where the party
flocked out of the glare into some little church.
And, seeing him shiver in this cool sanctuary,
just as I myself was doing, I turned
to him and asked, "Hedger? Chad? Are you
feeling *cold*?" And he said, "Cold? Well,, yes,
incredibly cold!" and "Me as well!" I said,
knowing that, unlike all the cautious others,
we'd both got ourselves sunstroke.'
                                   'Got it together,'
I didn't say but that was the story's point for me.
A meaningful one—yet surely without meaning also.
The two men murmur historic sympathy,
while the Merc edges us all on and up
nearer to what's brought about reunions
more complex and diverse even than ours today:
the stalwart cathedral, minatory, ultimate.

INTERLUDE

Small and neat, this attic bedsit,
the neatness he hadn't expected on
meeting its occupant at the front door
three storeys below, the sandy hair
tousled, eyes bloodshot at barely midday.
He himself was neat of course, had to be,
in black loose-fitting suit that went
with his smart black attaché case. 'Can you
kindly give me your attention for a few
moments? I've real good news to bring!'
'I never do things *kindly*, mate. And
whatever good news could *you* bring *me?*
But come on up!' And a steep long 'up' it was.
'Normally' the caller explains, 'we work
in pairs. But Mike took sick today,
and I figured I could bring our news alone
though it's against rules.' The room's single
window looks out over pantiled roofs
and severed trapeziums of mellow brick.
A huge jar of Gold Blend Decaff
presides from the room's one table
as with authority. 'Want some coff-coff?'
An ignorant question. 'We do not permit
ourselves stimulants.' Host barks a brief laugh;
'You're gonna kill me, mate, saying things like that;
this stuff's a *downer*—for fucked-up nerves!'
'Shall we get straight to business!' says the other
zipping case open with practised ease,
and out the music-stand and printed sheets come,
host watching as the pantiles' pigeons watch *him*,
curious, uninvolved. 'You heard of Utah?
You heard of Jesus Christ?'
                                        What else but nod?
'But have you heard of Joseph Smith? Way back
in 1830, in western New York State,
our founder was granted the honour of

receiving ancient American records
on plates of gold. And the truths he read there
he carried, persecuted but brave, across
great wilderness to the Promised Land.'
And now sheets placed on music-stand reveal
maps, diagrams, bright pictures of an Exodus…
'Isn't this *good* news?'
                            But all his host says,
but silently, is 'So here we go again!'
and peels his Man City T-shirt off his lean
body to reveal LOSERS TAKE ALL
tattooed on his chest.
                            'No, friend,
they do not!' says his guest, his saviour,
as if he'd heard, not read, the slogan.
'Before my year as a missionary I was
just riding cattle on my dad's lonely farm.
Then I moved on. And my heart grew glad,
and, friend, your heart can grow glad too!'

... AND FRIENDS (1)

He got up each weekday to North-of-England
mornings, the air damp but tangy like its people's
voices. He biked uphill from the white-washed, slate-
roofed farmhouse where he lodged to his clock-towered
work-place. Here the watching faces of the young
gave marks to his words, movements, actions,
sometimes with ticks, more often with crosses,
in classrooms glowing with regional pride,
some of them with views onto distant moors:
stretches of purple ignorant of examination grades.

They were not like he'd been at their age, his judges;
the North relishes itself. Going away from it
you try only with coming back in mind. After
his own Northern boyhood, a long southern exile
during which he constantly longed for elsewhere.
But to this place of his return such a pining
is a wrong: local teams, local beer, local mates,
with challenge enough here in limestone and stream.

But to him these all say—Be off again! Get away!

Fifth Form (V A) GCSE Eng Lit, a
favourite among his official work-sites:
'Today we've got a very interesting, and I think
a very *important* poem to read. By W.B. Yeats.
An Irish Airman Foresees His Death.'
Was it his word 'important' that galvanised
the twenty pupils before him, or that,
for some of the boys, who were Air Cadets
and who'd return jauntily truculent
from their weekly exercises in light-blue kit,
(sometimes their planes turned upside down
in the sky), *Airman* spelt a real possible call?
Anyhow they're all listening: girls jut heads
charmingly forwards, boys un-slouch themselves....

'This Irishman isn't political, he doesn't care
about nationalism, or competing ideals,
he knows only the places he's grown up in:
My country is Kiltartan Cross,
My countrymen Kiltartan's poor.
'Like we might say Nidderdale and Yoredale,'
says Ian Pringle, always quick. 'Exactly!'
his teacher agrees, 'just like that!..... Yet
there's another reason why he assents
to being up there, facing deadly fire in the sky;
does anyone see it?' But he chooses not to wait:
A lonely impulse of delight
Drove to this tumult in the clouds;
He could stop the reading here, but doesn't, goes on:
I balanced all, brought all to mind,
The years to come seemed waste of breath,
A waste of breath the years behind
In balance with this life, this death.

What length of time passed before,
later that term, quite unsolicited,
that secretive member of this class slouched
up to his desk, a smile in his brown eyes,
Hedger, Chad Hedger?..... Never later could he
quite place this moment in time, and most of his
life he had no reason for doing so!
By then too many dull days had formed a line
which he knew he shouldn't have found so dull,
feet inclined for a wilder walking, eyes that
scrutinised hill-tops for tempting outlines
of far-away ridges, trunk and groin which
told him of unfulfilled needs—he had grown
in thrall to all of these, obstinately so.

He now has guilty fears his lessons did indeed
grow dull alongside himself; maybe V A's
didn't. Yeats gave way to Owen, Sassoon,
Graves in the prescribed anthology, and

there was Dickens (*A Tale of Two Cities*—
what a choice!) and *Romeo and Juliet*.

His own mind was on the move; couldn't
the Anthropology of Claude Lévi-Strauss
expand his dim understanding of life? Each
morning now he'd swallow his farmhouse breakfast—
porridge with treacle and cream, scrambled eggs
and a hot buttered muffin with chunky marmalade—
as if he were about to jump on that bike of his
not for pupils but for *Tristes Tropiques*,
La Pensée Sauvage and *Mythologiques 1* and *11*,
the right territory for him, he now felt,
new, adventurous, but with the ancient in power.

Perhaps it was its enticing landscapes
his mind was viewing when he noticed
that figure moving toward his desk, on the dais
he wouldn't be mounting much longer; half-gauche,
but in the blazered, flannelled, narrow-eyed mien
was that same confidence with which he'd stripped
on the raft. In class Chad spoke little and softly. Now—
'I hear you're leaving us, sir!'—flat, toneless.
'Yes, that's right… Hedger. Chad. After two years
one's got to move on, they say.' (Oh, *did* they?)
'What to do *next*, that's the difficult thing!'
says Hedger, 'that's what I find! But *you*, sir…?'
Had Chad ever said so much to him since sun
in Poland? He let his last sentence trail off
but found more to say.
        'Is it still your view, sir,
that we should all aim for *a lonely impulse
of delight*? Even *among the clouds above*.
You gave us to think that the Irish airman
you read with us was right to believe it.
And since then it's what *I've* come to believe.
A lonely impulse of delight makes sense of everything.'

CHAD HEDGER AND FRIENDS

Here are men who believe the world began
in—and with—the blink of an eye,
and that's how this journey is beginning:
two of them, casually in dominance of
these seconds of time, push four rafts off,
one by one, onto the rush of white-water.
Meanwhile a cousin of theirs, ritualistically
dressed, river-water up to booted calves,
plays on his fiddle—double-stopping
like nothing you've listened to before
as if his chords are telegraphing
info from fierce-sunned sky to the
wide-brimmed hats of his fellows,
who, for three hours, one man per raft,
will see that you and your companions
are borne unstoppably forward through the gorge.
Never mind the risings into air over rapids,
or the narrow dodging of spiteful rocks,
these gypsy-men who know so much
know your journey has a civilised end.

And isn't the river somewhat like yourself, you
wonder, something you know a lot better since
being in Poland, and may know better still now
you're riding a raft down a border (with Slovakia).
You've a will that can help you make sense of
practically everything, but you see there's a wildness
inside you which doesn't want you to. Same as it
doesn't see why there should be *any* end
to this present journey. Seven loops
the Dunajec makes in this gorge,
but you're not able to count them, so busy
with swooshing, tossing water, any more than
you can the bumps in your life back home—
Mum breaking down in distress at Dad,
a maths problem not submitting to your mind,

a long-planned chatting-up blocked in the street—
and hadn't life gone on 'regardless' as they said,
like Eternity itself, that strange destination?

To which the limestone cliffs on either side
surely belong, so high, so invincible—
and what can these be, like interrogative marks
punctuating vertical sheets of near-white rock?
Sharing the raft with you and three mates
is the man from your school you facetiously
call Master. He sees the direction of your gaze.
'Storks,' he says, 'on every protrusion in the cliff.
Look at those wagon-wheels of sticks and straw!
Nests the storks themselves have made; on each
a couple of them is standing! They mate for life,
and their families—even when they're migrating
far south to Africa—are so harmonious
humans have looked up to them in envy
for millennia.' Mate for life, eh? Not like
Mum and Dad, perhaps not like yourself....
Your eyes travel to where stork couples can
be descried—well, just!—three and a half feet
tall, white-feathered, red bare legs, and a
stooping attitude not unlike your own
when caught off-guard. Master has more to say:
'Strain your eyes, Chad, but no real point
in straining your ears. Storks don't sing,
instead they snap beaks together, so that
clitter-clatter, clitter-clatter is what they say
to the world. Yet the ancients thought storks'
conversation was so interesting that
once you started listening to it, you'd never
want to leave the birds, you'd stay for Eternity.'

That does it, together with something else.
Master—a shy but talkative guy who stumbles
round the school in shabby casual clothes—
is now explaining how these birds find it hard
to take off so need to find a current of

warm air to lift their bodies up, and then
carry them sunwards to great heights.
'Me too,' you mumble, though it's not clear
even to yourself with which statement
you're agreeing. The sun is at its strongest
in this cloudless sky, and the river is surely
sun-water as it hisses and speeds along.
So you pull off T-shirt and display your
bare chest to the winged question-marks above.
A few moments later and, glancing
behind you, why, bloody hell, you see
Master has done like you. And the rafts
(you're in Number Three) seem pleased
with you both: another bend, another rapid,
another flat wheel of a nest on the cliff-face.

What burns chills!; during your embrace
of the sun, heat is not your only
visitor. Mercury, the winged messenger
of the gods, nearer to the sun than any
other heavenly body, is both the hottest and
the coldest planet of the batch.
When loops straighten out and cliffs shrink
into banks, and the rafts slow down on
a calmed current, you can't make out
what it is that's happening to you.
Szczawnica arrives—impossible for it not to.
The whole company makes a ragged way
to its tourist-sights. Inside a little church
your Master notices you, says: 'Hedger? Chad?
are you feeling *cold*?' How through your
shivers could you not reply: 'Well, yes,
incredibly cold!' And Master tells you
'Me as well!' and then you know that
for some reason the two of you are one,
heat with cold, sense with fear, life with death.

And in all the varieties of temperature
ahead of you, you never cease to feel at your
back those gypsies by the Polish river
enabling your journey by shoving
the rafts off, and holding in their heads
a history of the world, of life-forms,
you can't, with what you now know, reject.

... AND FRIENDS (2)

The woods in southern Poland were rich
that summer in wild strawberries,
small, sharp, sweet. Girls wearing light
cotton dresses reached arms up to
overhanging boughs, their hands plucked
leaves to put on their noses: folded ovals
of greenness to ward off the intolerant sun.

And you, Chad, who after your river-ride
knew that intolerance better than did your
mates, asked Siobhan Malley to pause a
moment as the lot of you exchanged woods
for a hill-path to a famous look-out.
'I want to give you *this*!' you said (you'd already
taken her by the hand a few times during
steep twists up the slopes). With a smile in eyes
but not on mouth, you placed a lime-leaf,
which you'd just picked yourself, on her button nose.
'*That'll* keep you beautiful!' you told her.

It was this tableau of all those with Chad at centre
that came back to me first when, dreaming
over my laptop, I travelled through my long-past
years in a small northern cathedral city.
But as more pictures followed, I sensed a changing
in me, that compelled me to see and hear what,
sunk in self, I hadn't then responded to enough.
Chad became all at once immense in stature....
I should know about him *now*, find the shape
he'd made of life. Here surely would be lessons
for myself to learn—from Yorkshire, Poland
and this youth who'd kept himself mysterious
(or had done so at least to me).
                    Our whole planet
hangs over computer keyboards. But it took
but a minute and a half to find him—among the

obituaries—and only two or three more
to discover he'd taken his own life.

And now change in me of another kind began. Later
I'd go back to that city where I'd been (to him)
'Master', meet mates of his and that geography
teacher who'd organised our Poland trip,
who now was blind yet as attached to the walks
and monuments of his Yorkshire home
as he had ever been.
                        But you can't—not yet—
penetrate Death to learn what you thirst
after knowing while still unable (unwilling?)
to name it all? So there are poems to write.

ETRUSCAN WITNESS

Paparazzi skirmish
for shots of me
as I saunter into street
in Armani glasses;
their flashes vie with
lit-up signs, Nutella,
Zanussi, Mercedes-Benz,
while cathedral bells,
call a glutted citizenry
to evening Mass.

Why such attention?
Some kindness of mine
judged newsworthy?
Some repeated one-liner?
A handsome scratch-card win?

I now feel that brash, exotic
glare and swank 'd be
no worse for my soul
(street-wise despite itself)
than year-after-year
of country obscurity
and this growing heap
of yellowing internet
print-outs of kingdoms
that went under.

I've voyaged, I see, too
far beyond that ancient
revered and baffling alphabet.
I know what forced its vanished makers
to send up birds as signs
while double-pipes were playing
along with barbiton and curved trumpet.

'If you can't beat 'em, join 'em!'
Let those twelve cities rest,
and their power-wielding women
lie as daunting memories in tufa-built
tombs shaped like beehives
on antique hills of farmed tranquillity.

I tried over-hard to broadcast
the culture which, uniquely,
believed all peoples were timed.
Thus they could never outstay
our world's unstable welcome;
I hoped my news would earn
me thanks. Wrong, well, almost!
Are you listening there
in those bleak but glistening
wastes to the east of
Canary Wharf? Probably not,
but Paparazzi, here I come!

SOLITUDE: AN AMBIGUITY

Landlubbers sob on heaving bunks
while albatrosses, silvered by sun,
follow the choppy wakes of ships.
An impatient young man in a travel-ad
piazza feels itching in the groin as
varied couples pass him, then shrugs his
back-pack higher. In a pet-shop
a puma with abstracted, vengeful face
howls against his price-tagged bars.

You, I know, still back home in summer,
are seeing great golden eggs
all over our lawn, and among them,
blood-smeared feathers telling us
our laying goose is dead. You stretch out
toes to touch Aladdin's lamp, rusty
after night-vapours, its genie gone.
You yourself linger at our garden gate,
barefoot, in boxer shorts, all dreams over,
squashing brilliant dew-drops with your heel.

You might still be seeing off (or letting out)
another night-companion, who, after cross-legged
hours on cushion-strewn floor, syncopated
creeds and dicta with you.
                       Single again, much-
travelled, I've come to know that albatrosses
are snared by unseen sub-surface wires
from state-of-the-art trawlers on southern seas.

Time to shower and get dressed, garden's empty
though moist with doubt. It's an indigo
puma who pads by your wall; in the pet-shop
the tawny one has a paw caught fast. A fact:
pumas weep tears when Death is threatening.

AN IRISH AIRMAN FORESEES HIS DEATH

I know that I shall meet my fate
Somewhere among the clouds above;
Those that I fight I do not hate,
Those that I guard I do not love;
My country is Kiltartan Cross,
My countrymen Kiltartan's poor,
No likely end could bring them loss
Or leave them happier than before.
Nor law, nor duty bade me fight,
Nor public men, nor cheering crowds,
A lonely impulse of delight
Drove to this tumult in the clouds;
I balanced all, brought all to mind,
The years to come seemed waste of breath ,
A waste of breath the years behind
In balance with this life, this death.

– W.B. Yeats 1918/1919